Bob Chilcott

Songbook

9 SONGS FOR MIXED VOICES

T0057492

MUSIC DEPARTMENT

OXFORD
UNIVERSITY PRESS

OXFORD
UNIVERSITY PRESS

Great Clarendon Street, Oxford OX2 6DP, England
198 Madison Avenue, New York, NY, 10016, USA

Oxford University Press is a department of the University of Oxford.
It furthers the University's aim of excellence in research, scholarship,
and education by publishing worldwide

Oxford is a registered trade mark of Oxford University Press
in the UK and in certain other countries

© Oxford University Press 2006

Bob Chilcott has asserted his right under the Copyright, Designs
and Patents Act, 1988, to be identified as the Composer of these Works

Database right Oxford University Press (maker)

First published 2006

All rights reserved. No part of this publication may be reproduced,
stored in a retrieval system, or transmitted, in any form or by any means,
without the prior permission in writing of Oxford University Press,
or as expressly permitted by law. Enquiries concerning reproduction
outside the scope of the above should be sent to the Music Copyright
Department, Oxford University Press, at the address above

Permission to perform the works in this anthology in public
(except in the course of divine worship) should normally be obtained
from the Performing Right Society Ltd. (PRS), 29/33 Berners Street,
London W1T 3AB, or its affiliated Societies in each country throughout
the world, unless the owner or the occupier of the premises
being used holds a licence from the Society

Permission to make a recording must be obtained in advance
from the Mechanical-Copyright Protection Society Ltd. (MCPS),
Elgar House, 41 Streatham High Road, London SW16 1ER,
or its affiliated Societies in each country throughout the world

ISBN 978-0-19-335571-2

Music origination by Enigma Music Production Services, Amersham, Bucks.
Printed in Great Britain on acid-free paper by
Halstan & Co. Ltd., Amersham, Bucks.

Contents

Aka-Tonbo	4
Ar Hyd y Nos	8
Composed upon Westminster Bridge, September 3, 1802	12
Dance in the Street	18
O Danny boy	30
Over the Wave	35
The Lily and the Rose	42
The Runner	52
The Skye Boat Song	65

Composer's note

This collection includes a mixture of both original pieces and arrangements. 'Aka-Tonbo' dates back to 1983, and was originally written for the vocal group The Light Blues for their tour of Japan. 'The Runner' is taken from a set entitled *The Modern Man I Sing*, composed in 1990, and was written for the choir of Gustavus Adolphus College, Minnesota. It was my very first paid commission for an original choral work! 'Composed upon Westminster Bridge', 'Dance in the Street', and 'Over the Wave' are also taken from larger works, and 'The Lily and The Rose' is a reworking of a piece that I originally wrote for children's choir. The three folksong arrangements, 'Ar Hyd y Nos', 'The Skye Boat Song', and 'O Danny boy' were written to be featured within the famous *Fantasia on British Sea Songs* by Henry Wood, and were first performed at the BBC Last Night of the Proms in 2005.

I am very grateful to Jane Griffiths for her work on this volume.

Aka-Tonbo

Rofuu Miki
(1889-1964)

KOSAKU YAMADA
(1886-1965)
arr. BOB CHILCOTT
(b. 1955)

*Keyboard reduction for rehearsal only.

English prose translation:
The red dragonflies fly at sunset. When I was young, and riding on nanny's back, I saw them. We picked mulberry fruits into a little basket in the field of a mountain. Or was it just a dream? At fifteen she married and was gone. Letters never seemed to come. The red dragonflies fly at sunset. Look, one now rests on a bamboo stick.

This piece is also available arranged for SAB *a cappella* in *Songstream 1: 10 Songs for Youth Choirs* (ISBN 978–0–19–343545–2).

© Oxford University Press 2005 and 2006. Photocopying this copyright material is ILLEGAL.

Printed in Great Britain

OXFORD UNIVERSITY PRESS, MUSIC DEPARTMENT, GREAT CLARENDON STREET, OXFORD OX2 6DP
Photocopying this copyright material is ILLEGAL.

12
ha-ta-ke - no ku-wa-no - mi - o, ko-ka-go - ni tsu-n-da - wa
(mm)
(mm)
17
S.
ma-bo-ro - shi - ka.
mp
Ju - go - de ne - ya - wa yo-me-ni-yu-
A.
(mm)
p
oo
T.
(mm)
p
oo
B.
mp
Ju - go - de ne - ya - wa yo-me-ni-yu-
mp

23
- ki, o - sa - to - no ta - yo - ri - mo ta - e ha - te - ta.
(oo)
(oo)
- ki, o - sa - to - no ta - yo - ri - mo ta - e ha - te - ta.
28
p
Yu - ya - ke ko - ya - ke - no
pp
pp
(oo)
mm
mm
pp
pp
(oo)
mm
pp
mm
pp

33
a-ka-to - n - bo, to-ma - te i - ru - yo sa-o-no - sa -
(mm)
mm
(mm)
(mm)
38
- ki.
mm
(mm)
mm
(mm)
mm
(mm)
mm

for the BBC Last Night of the Proms 2005
and dedicated to Serendipity and the BBC Symphony Chorus

Ar Hyd y Nos

John Ceiriog Hughes (1832–87)
English words: Sir Harold Boulton (1859–1935)

Welsh trad.
arr. BOB CHILCOTT

The orchestral accompaniment for this arrangement is available to hire from the publisher.

© Oxford University Press 2005 and 2006. Photocopying this copyright material is ILLEGAL.

12
div.
mp
mf
dim.
S.
A.
nos.
night.
Go - lau ar - all yw ty - wy - llwch, I ar - ddan - gos
Soft the drow - sy hours are creep - ing, Hill and vale in
T.
B.
mp
mf
dim.
mp
mf
dim.
16
p dolce
gwir bryd - fer - thwch, Teu - lu'r ne - foedd mewn ta - wel - wch,
slum - ber sleep - ing, I my lov - ing vi - gil keep - ing,
p dolce
p dolce
19
Ar hyd y nos.
All through the night.
mf
dim.

23
unis. p
O mor si - riol gwe - na se - ren,
While the moon her watch is keep - ing,
p
26
p
Ar hyd y nos,
All through the night,
Ar hyd y nos.
All through the night.
I o - le - uo'i
While the wea - ry
29
ar hyd y nos.
all through the night.
chwaer ddae - a - ren, Ar hyd y nos.
world is sleep - ing, All through the night.

32
mp
mf
dim.
Nos yw he - naint pan ddaw cy - studd, Ond i har - ddu dyn a'i hwyr - ddydd,
O'er thy spi - rit gent - ly steal - ing, Vi - sions of de - light re - veal - ing,
mp
mf
dim.
mp
mf
dim.
36 unis.
p
Rhown ein go - lau gwan i'n gi - lydd, Ar hyd y
Breathes a pure and ho - ly feel - ing, All through the
p
p
39
rit.
nos.
night.
rit.
pp

Composed upon Westminster Bridge, September 3, 1802

William Wordsworth (1770–1850) BOB CHILCOTT

This piece is also available in an arrangement for SATB and two pianos as the fourth movement of *Songs and Cries of London Town* (ISBN 978–0–19–343297–0).

© Oxford University Press 2001 and 2006. Photocopying this copyright material is ILLEGAL.

11
poco cresc.
soul who could pass by a sight so touch-ing in its ma-jes-ty:
poco cresc.
15
p
This Ci-ty now doth like a gar-ment wear the
p
mp
mp
18
beau-ty of the morn-ing;
mp espress.
p

22
p
Si - lent, bare, Ships, to - wers, domes,
p

26
mp cresc.
the - a - tres and tem-ples lie o - pen un-to the fields and to the
mp cresc.
mp cresc.

29
f
mp dolce e dim.
sky;
All bright and glit-ter-ing in the smoke - less
mp dolce e dim.
f
All bright and glit-ter-ing in the
f
mp dolce
poco rit.
a tempo
32
p espress.
air.
Ne-ver did sun more
smoke - less air.
poco rit.
a tempo
p espress.
35
S.
A.
beau-ti-ful-ly steep in his first splen-dour val-ley, rock, or hill;

38
p dolce
poco rit.
T.
B.
Ne'er_ saw I, ne-ver felt, a calm so deep!
dolce
a tempo
42
p semplice
46
poco rit.
a tempo
p
S.
A.
The ri - ver gli-deth at his
T.
B.
p
poco rit.
a tempo

50
poco rit.
own sweet will; Dear God! the ve - ry hou - ses seem a -
poco rit.
mp
mp dolce
53
a little slower
- sleep; and all that migh - ty heart is ly - ing
a little slower
56
pp
rit.
still!
pp
rit.

for the Vasari Singers
in celebration of their 21st anniversary

Dance in the Street

Paul Verlaine (1844–96)
Free trans. by Bob Chilcott

BOB CHILCOTT

This is No. 1 of two pieces entitled *Dances in the Streets*. Both pieces, set to the original French by Paul Verlaine, are available separately (ISBN 978–0–19–343334–2).

© Oxford University Press 2001 and 2006. Photocopying this copyright material is ILLEGAL.

9
mp
danc - ing, danc - ing, danc - ing, we're danc - ing, danc - ing, danc - ing, we're
mf
Danc - ing, we're danc - ing, danc - ing, we're danc - ing,
mp
13
mf
He has a good look in his eye, Bright as the stars up in the sky,
mp
Danc - ing, oh, oh
danc - ing, danc - ing, danc - ing, we're danc - ing, danc - ing, danc - ing, we're
mp
danc - ing, we're danc - ing, danc - ing, we're danc - ing,
mf
mp

17
cresc.
He makes me smile, I don't know why, as we dance in the street!
danc - ing,
danc - ing, danc - ing, danc - ing, we're danc - ing, danc - ing, dance in the
danc - ing, we're danc - ing, danc - ing, dance in the street!
21
f
La la lul lul la la la la la lul lul lul la la la
La lul lul la lul lul la la la la lul lul la lul lul la la la
street! la la la la la
La la la la la la

25
mf
la la lul lul lul la la la la la lul lul lul la lul lul la! We're
la la lul lul lul la la la la lul lul la lul lul la lul lul la!
la la la la lul la!
la la la la lul la!
mf
29
mp
danc-ing, danc-ing, danc-ing, we're danc-ing, danc-ing, danc-ing, we're danc - ing, danc - ing,
mf
mp
Danc - ing, we're danc - ing, danc - ing, we're danc - ing, danc - ing, we're
mf
She has a way of
mp
Danc - ing,
mp
mf
mp

34
danc - ing, we're danc - ing, danc - ing, danc - ing, we're danc - ing, danc - ing,
danc - ing, danc - ing, we're danc - ing, danc - ing, we're
teas - ing me, Mov-ing a-round so ea - si - ly, She is a sight for
oh, oh danc - ing,
38
cresc.
f
danc - ing, we're danc - ing, danc - ing, dance in the street! La
danc - ing, danc - ing, dance in the street! La lul lul la lul lul
all to see as we dance in the street! La la lul lul
La la

42
la la la la la la la la la
la la la la lul lul la lul lul la la la la la lul lul lul
la la la la la lul lul lul la la la la la lul lul lul
la la la la la la la la la
46
la la la la la lul lul la!
mf
la la la la lul lul la lul lul la lul lul la! We're danc - ing,
mf
la la la la la lul lul lul la lul lul la! Danc - ing, we're
la la lul la!
mf

50
mp
Danc - ing,
mp
we're danc - ing, we're danc - ing, we're
mp
danc - ing, danc - ing, we're danc - ing, danc - ing, we're danc - ing,
f
And for a while the eve-ning calms,
mp
f
55
oh, oh danc - ing, we're
danc - ing, we're danc - ing, we're
danc - ing, we're danc - ing, danc - ing, we're danc - ing,
Smil-ing I hold her in my arms, Ho-ping she'll give in to my charms as we

59
cresc.
f
danc - ing, dance in the street! La la
danc - ing, dance in the street! La lul lul la lul lul la la la
danc - ing. La la lul lul la la la
dance in the street! La la la
63
la la la la la la la la
la lul lul la lul lul la la la la la lul lul lul la la la
la la lul lul lul la la la la la lul lul lul la la la
la la la la la la

67
mf
la la la la lul lul la! We're danc-ing, danc-ing, danc-ing, we're danc-ing, danc-ing,
mf
la lul lul la lul lul la lul lul la! We're danc - ing, danc - ing, we're
la la lul lul lul la lul lul la!
la lul la!
mf
72
mp
danc - ing, we're danc - ing, danc - ing, danc - ing, we're danc - ing, danc - ing,
mp
danc - ing, we're danc - ing, danc - ing, we're
f
Now as I look back to that time, Think-ing a - bout that
f
Now as I look back to that time, Think-ing a - bout that
mp
f

76
danc - ing, we're danc - ing, danc - ing, danc - ing, we're danc - ing, danc - ing,
danc - ing, we're danc - ing, danc - ing,
girl so fine, Oh, how I'd like to make her mine as we dance in the
girl so fine, Oh, how I'd like to make her mine as we dance in the
80
f
dance in the street! La la la la la
f
dance in the street! La lul lul la lul lul la la la la lul lul la lul lul
f
street! La la lul lul la la la la la lul lul lul
f
street! La la la la
f

84
la la la la la la la la la
la la la la la lul lul lul la la la la lul lul la lul lul
la la la la la lul lul lul la la la la la lul lul lul
la la la la la la
88
ff
S.1
la lul lul la la la la la la la
S.2
la lul lul la la la la la lul lul la la la la la lul lul lul
A.
la lul lul la la lul lul la lul lul la la la la lul lul la lul lul
T.
la lul lul la lul lul la la la la
B.
lul la la la la la

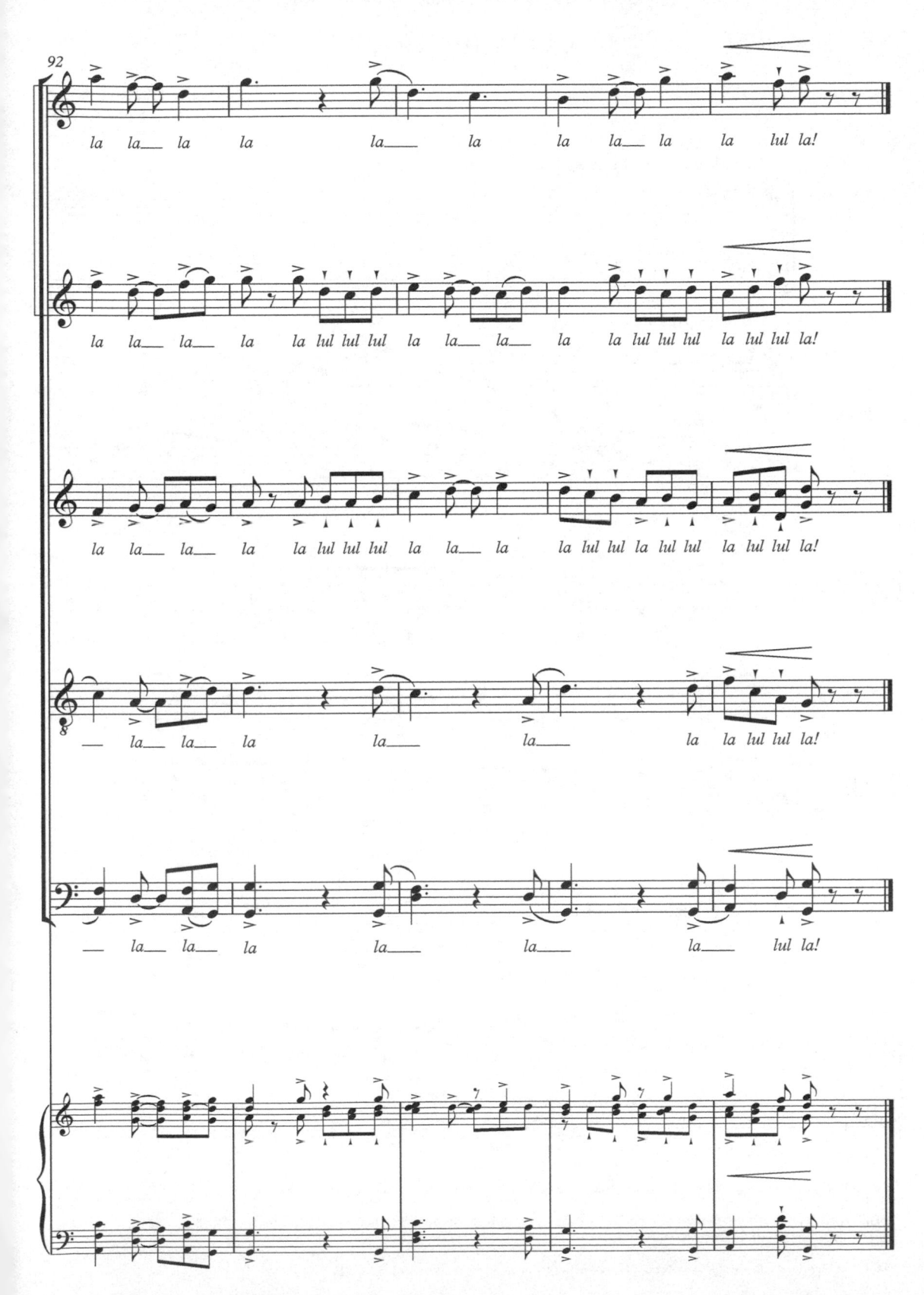
92
la la la la la la la la la la lul la!
la la la la la lul lul lul la la la la la lul lul lul la lul lul la!
la la la la la lul lul lul la la la la lul lul la lul lul la lul lul la!
la la la la la la la la la lul lul la!
la la la la la la la lul la!

for the BBC Last Night of the Proms 2005
and dedicated to Codetta and the BBC Symphony Chorus

O Danny boy

Fred Weatherly (1848–1929)

County Derry melody
arr. BOB CHILCOTT

The orchestral accompaniment for this arrangement is available to hire from the publisher.

An alternative arrangement of this piece for SATB and piano (entitled 'Londonderry Air') is available in *Encores for Choirs 1* (ISBN 978–0–19–343630–5).

© Oxford University Press 2005 and 2006. Photocopying this copyright material is ILLEGAL.

9
gone, and all the ro - ses fall - ing, 'tis you, 'tis you must go and I must
12
div.
mf
S.
A.
bide. But come ye back when sum-mer's in the mea - dow, Or when the
T.
B.
mf
mf
15
val - ley's hushed and white with snow, 'Tis I'll be there in sun-shine or in
f
f
f

18
dim.
mp
sha - dow. O Dan - ny boy, O Dan - ny boy I love you
dim.
mp
dim.
mp
20
so.
3
3
23
p
Dan - ny
unis. mp
And when you come and all the flowers are dy - ing, If I am

26
boy, O Dan-ny boy, Dan - ny boy.
dead, as dead I well may be, You'll come and find the place where I am
29
mp dolce
Dan - ny boy, O Dan-ny boy. And I shall
div.
ly - ing, And kneel and say an A - ve there for me.
mp dolce
32
cresc.
hear tho' soft you tread a - bove me, And all my grave will warm-er, sweet-er
cresc.
mp cresc.

35
f
dim.
unis.
be, For you will bend and tell me that you love me, And I shall
38
mp
p
sleep in peace un - til you come to me, you come to
41
rit.
pp
me.

Over the Wave

Native American (Ojibwa)

BOB CHILCOTT

This piece is from *Circlesong: a life cycle based on Native American writings*, scored for SAB choir, SATB choir, two pianos, and percussion. The full work is available to hire from the publisher.

© Oxford University Press 2003 and 2006. Photocopying this copyright material is ILLEGAL.

7
poco cresc.
rip - ples glow. But I've a charm that can make thee, dear, Steal
poco cresc.
poco cresc.
10
o - ver the wave to thy lo - ver here.
dolce
p
cresc.

14
rit.
a tempo
mf espress.
Who, maid-en, makes this ri - ver flow? The
mf espress.
rit.
a tempo
f dim.
mf espress.
18
poco cresc.
Spi - rit, he makes its rip - ples glow. Yet e - very blush that my
poco cresc.
poco cresc.

21
S.
A.
T.
B.
f
mf espress.
love would hide, Is mir-ror'd for me in the tell-tale tide. And
24
though thou sleep on the far-thest isle, Round which these dimp-ling
though thou sleep, thou sleep, the wa - ters
And though thou sleep on the far - thest
though thou sleep, the wa - ters

27
wa - ters smile. Yet I've a charm that can make thee, dear, Steal
smile. I've a charm that can make thee, Steal
isle, the wa - ters smile. I've a charm that can make thee Steal
smile. A charm, I've a charm, Steal
30
poco rit.
o - ver the wave to thy lo - ver here.
o - ver the wave to thy lo - ver here.
o - ver the wave to thy lo - ver here.
o - ver the wave to thy lo - ver here.
poco rit.
dim.
p

34
rit.
a tempo
p
mm
p
mm
p
mm
mp espress.
Who, maid-en, makes this ri - ver flow? The
rit.
a tempo
p espress.
38
(mm)
But I've a charm that can
(mm)
But I've a charm that can
(mm)
But I've a charm that can
p
Spi - rit, he makes its rip - ples glow. But I've a charm that can

41
poco rit.
a little slower
mp
make thee, dear, Steal o - ver the wave to thy
make thee, dear, o - ver the wave to thy
make thee, dear, o - ver the wave to thy
make thee, dear, o - ver the wave to thy
poco rit.
a little slower
44
rit.
pp
lo - ver here.
lo - ver here.
lo - ver here.
lo - ver here.
rit.
mp
pp

This SATB version for Peter Hunt and the Berkshire Youth Choir

The Lily and the Rose

Anon. 16th-cent. English

BOB CHILCOTT

The original version of this piece, scored for upper voices and piano, is also available (ISBN 978–0–19–343317–5).

© Oxford University Press 2002 and 2006. Photocopying this copyright material is ILLEGAL.

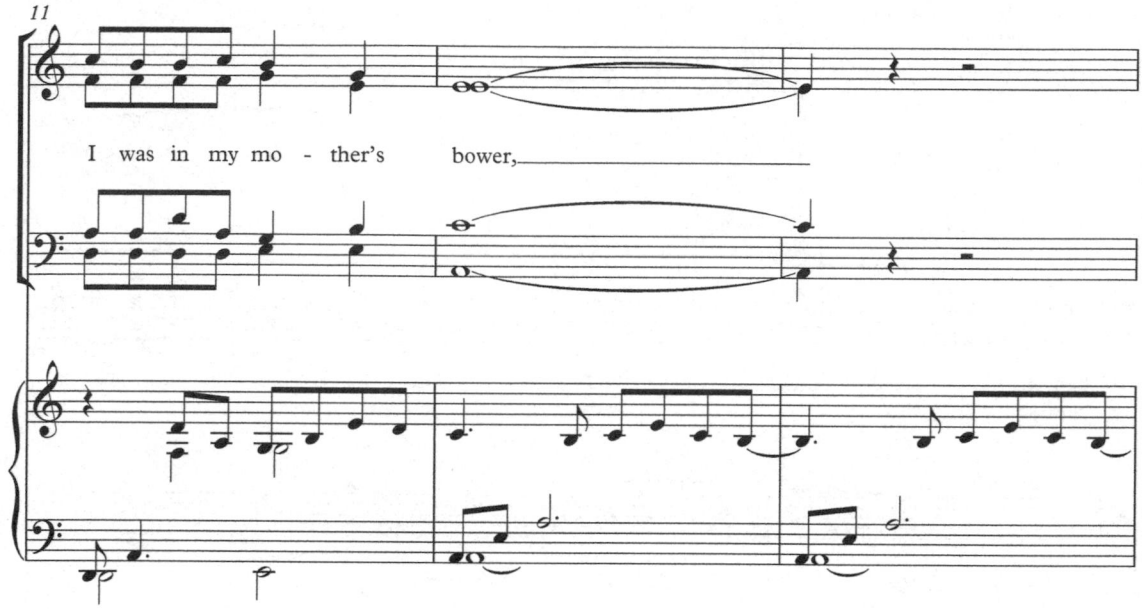
11
I was in my mo - ther's bower,

14
poco cresc.
The maid-ens came When I was in my mo - ther's bower, I
poco cresc.
poco cresc.

17
mp
had all that I would.
p dolce
had all that I would. The bai - ley bear - eth the
had, I had all that I would. The bai - ley bear - eth,
had all that I would.
The bai - ley, the bai - ley
mp
p dolce
mp
p dolce
20
poco cresc.
mp
bell a - way; The li - ly, the rose, the rose I lay. The
poco cresc.
mp
bear - eth the bell a - way; The li - ly, the rose I lay. The
poco cresc.

23
bai - ley bear - eth the bell a - way; The li - ly, the rose, the
bai - ley bear - eth,
bai - ley, the bai - ley bear - eth the bell, the bell a - way; The li - ly, the
mp
26
rose I lay.

30
S.
A.
T.
B.
mp più espress.
The sil-ver is white,
The sil - ver is
The sil - ver, the sil - ver is
The sil - ver is white,
33
red is the gold;
white, red is the gold, red is the gold, is the gold, the
white, red, red is the gold, red is the gold, the
red is the gold, red is the

36
The sil-ver is white, red is the gold; The
gold; the sil - ver is white, red is the gold, the gold; The
gold; the sil - ver is white, red is, red is the gold; The
gold; the sil - ver is white, red is the gold; The
39
mf
mp
S.
A.
robes they lay in fold. The
robes, the robes they lay in fold. The
T.
B.
robes they lay in fold. The
mf
mp
mf

41
bai - ley bear - eth the bell a - way; The li - ly, the rose, the
bai - ley bear - eth,
bai - ley, the bai - ley bear - eth the bell a - way; The li - ly, the
mp
44
poco cresc.
mf
rose I lay. The bai - ley bear - eth the bell a - way; The
bai - ley bear - eth, bear - eth the bell, the bell a -
rose I lay. The bai - ley, the bai - ley bear - eth the bell, the bell a -
poco cresc.
mf
poco cresc.
mf

47
li - ly, the rose, the rose I lay.
And
- way;
- way; The li - ly, the rose I lay.

poco più mosso
51
f
through the glass win - dows shines the sun.
f
poco più mosso
f

54
f espress.
molto dim.
S.
How_ should I love, How_ should I love, and I so
A.
How,___ How_ should I love,___ How_ should I love, and I so
T.
How should I, How_ should I love,___ How_ should I love, and I so
B.
How should I love, I love, should I love, and I so
57
poco rit.
p
pp sempre
tempo I
young, so___ young?___
The bai - ley___ bear - eth the
The bai - ley___ bear - eth,___
The bai - ley, the bai - ley___

61
bell a - way; The li - ly, the rose, the rose I lay. The
bear - eth the bell a - way; The li - ly, the rose I lay. The
64
bai - ley bear - eth the bell a - way; The li - ly, the rose, the
bai - ley bear - eth,
bai - ley, the bai - ley bear - eth the bell, the bell a - way; The li - ly, the
67
molto rit.
slower
rose, the rose I lay.
molto rit.
slower

for Karle Erickson and the Gustavus Choir

The Runner

Walt Whitman (1819–92)

BOB CHILCOTT

*Breathe in and out through mouth or nose, starting with an out breath, never too forcefully. Stop and start ad lib.

© Oxford University Press 2006. Photocopying this copyright material is ILLEGAL.

*Keyboard reduction for rehearsal only.

15
He is lean and_ sin - ew -
He is lean and_ sin - ew -
18
-y with mus - cu-lar legs.
-y with mus - cu-lar legs.
mf
huh uh

21
He is thin - ly clothed, he
huh uh huh uh huh uh huh uh huh uh (etc.)
He is thin - ly clothed, he
23
leans for - ward as he runs, With
leans for - ward as he runs, With

26
light - ly closed fists and arms part - ial - ly
light - ly closed fists and arms part - ial - ly
29
raised.
raised.
mf
huh uh huh uh

32
f
On a flat road, on a
f
On a flat road,
(etc.)
mf
35
flat road runs the
on a flat road

37
well - trained run - ner, runs the
runs the well - trained run - ner,
39
well - trained run - ner,
runs the well - trained run - ner,

41
run-ner,
run-ner,
run-ner,
run-ner,
44
run-ner,
ff
run-ner, run-ner, run-ner, run-ner, run-ner,
run-ner,
ff
run-ner, run-ner, run-ner, run-ner, run-ner,
ff

47
a niente
S.
run-ner, run-ner.
a niente
T.
run-ner, run-ner.
div.
p
na na na na (etc.)
p
B.
50
A.
div.
p
na na na (etc.)
cresc. (to bar 59)
T.
cresc. (to bar 59)
53
mp
A.
mf
mp
T.
mf
mf cresc. (to bar 59)
div.
B.
na na na na (etc.)
mp cresc. (to bar 59)
mf

56
f
f
f
f
59
ff
S.
na na na na (etc.)
ff
A.
ff
T.
ff
B.
ff

61
dim. (until bar 77)
dim. (until bar 73)
dim. (until bar 69)
dim. (until end)
dim.
63
f
f
f
f
f

65
mf
huh uh huh uh (etc.)
67
mf
mf
mf
a niente
mf

70
S.
A.
B.
mp
mp
mp
73
pp dim.
a niente
pp dim.
76
a niente
S.
B.
79
B.
a niente

for the BBC Last Night of the Proms 2005
and dedicated to the BBC Singers and the National Youth Choir of Scotland

The Skye Boat Song

Sir Harold Boulton
(1859–1935)

Scottish trad.
arr. BOB CHILCOTT

The orchestral accompaniment for this arrangement is available to hire from the publisher.

© Oxford University Press 2005 and 2006. Photocopying this copyright material is ILLEGAL.

13
mp
S.
A.
Car - ry the lad that is born to be
T.
B.
Car - ry the lad that is born to be king,
17
king, O - ver the sea to Skye!
O - ver the sea to Skye!
21 unis. f
Loud the winds howl, loud the waves roar, Thun - der-claps
f
f

26
div.
rend the air, Baf - fled our foes
div.
31
stand on the shore, fol - low they will not dare.
they will not dare.
37
mf
Speed bon - nie boat, like a bird on the wing,
mf
mf

41
On - ward the sail - ors cry!
45
Car - ry the lad that is born to be king,
49
O - ver the sea to Skye!

53
mp dolce
Though the waves leap, soft shall ye
unis.
mp dolce
Though the waves leap, soft shall ye sleep,
mp dolce
57
a ro - yal bed;
sleep, a ro - yal, a ro - yal bed;
O - cean's a ro - yal bed;
61
Rocked in the deep, Flo - ra will
Rocked in the deep, Flo - ra will keep

65
keep watch by your wea - ry head.
watch by your wea - ry head.
69 unis.
p
Speed bon-nie boat, like a bird on the wing,
p
p
73
On - ward the sail - ors cry!

77
Car - ry the lad that is born to be king, O - ver the
82
sea to Skye!
87
rit.
rit.
pp